W0082211

A GREAT AMERICAN
Love Story

JACK KELLY

A Great American Love Story

© 2022 Jack Kelly

All rights reserved. No part of this publication may be reproduced, distributed, or
transmitted in any form or by any means, including photocopying, recording, or other
electronic or mechanical methods, without the prior written permission of the publisher,
except in the case of brief quotations embodied in critical reviews and certain other non-
commercial uses permitted by copyright law.

Print ISBN: 978-1-66781-560-2
eBook ISBN: 978-1-66781-561-9

Only in America could a boy from western New York, who never left his neighborhood until the age of 18, could a life like mine be possible. Only in America could a girl like Ingrid, a child of war, enter the country, alone, from Germany at the age of 21 with only the clothes on her back, imagine the life she would have. Together, the unimaginable became a reality. It was meant to be. Ingrid's and my journey is a true love story – with our great country and with each other. I hope you enjoy it.

THE EARLY YEARS

My name is John Brian Patrick Kelly (JB to my old Cornell friends). Patrick came at confirmation. I was born on Flag Day, June 14th, 1936 at the depth of the "Great Depression." My birthplace was St. Mary's Hospital, Niagara Falls, New York. My Dad had retained his job during the depression with the Loyalty Group Insurance Company. He was an insurance adjuster. He hated his job every day of his life but he did it. The most salary he ever made was $9,500 a year when he retired after 47 years. Dad's Mom died when he was 4 from tuberculosis. Dad struggled through his teenage years in Syracuse. He became a fine golfer, learning as a caddie in Syracuse. He loved his golf.

Mom was raised by my Grandmother who maintained the family as a single mom during the depression. After Mom and Dad married, Gram lived with us for the rest of her life.

We moved seven or eight times from one flat to another during the war years in Niagara Falls. My Dad really wanted to buy our house on Wyoming Avenue in Niagara Falls. The price was $6,500 and Dad couldn't come up with the down payment in 1939.

We moved many times during the war years. The husband of the neighbor in the flat above was killed with the U.S. Army in France. Rose Winsko was the widow's name. Jerry was her son. We had food and gas rationing. I think Dad only got 3 gallons of gas a week. Maybe he got 5. Our one outing was a drive to Lewiston, New York, to Hibbard's Frozen Custard stand. We got 10¢ single cones. They were great.

My sister, Karen, was born in 1941 and my brother, Rob, in 1945. We were still living in a flat. We had pails of sand in the attic in case of enemy attack. A kerosene stove kept us warm in winter.

One of my earliest memories was sitting at the dining room table Sunday morning, December 7th, 1941. Dad leaped up from the table and knelt down by an old Philco radio we had. I remember being with him when he heard the news of the Pearl Harbor surprise attack by the Japanese. Dad tried to enlist as a medic but he was too old.

The war years ended with the atomic bomb being dropped on Hiroshima and then Nagasaki. I remember the headlines.

Niagara Falls was an old industrial city. The industry was built on cheap power from the Falls. The city is on the border of Canada. The area has been depressed for generations. The weather is very cold, and the seasons are short except for winter. The people are hardworking but the opportunities are few.

Through the war years I grew up going to several different public schools. I walked to school. I loved to read and early on read the classic boys' adventure stories, Tom Swift etc. I took a test in the 4th grade which put me in a special "informal group" for 5th and 6th grade. We had a great teacher, Miss Hall. We took French and had an imaginative time. As O'Reilly says in "Old School" lots of _____ _____ and no appetizers." I only remember the family going out to dinner once and that was to a local diner.

My Dad and Mom would take a cottage for a week or two at Niagara on the Lake for vacation. I remember spending time with the Canadian soldiers manning their guard station overlooking Lake Ontario. Lots of young women were at Niagara on the Lake too. They were helping with the farm war production.

I started early selling creams door-to-door, mowing lawns and shoveling lots of snow.

When the war ended, Dad would take me to basketball games in Buffalo at the Memorial Auditorium at the foot of Buffalo Avenue on Lake Erie. Great games, but it was the coldest place in the world on Saturday night with the wind blowing across Lake Erie from Canada.

Dad was a great baseball fan too. We would walk to the Niagara Falls Citizens games (Class C) at Hyde Park Stadium, (adult tickets 65¢, and children were 25¢). I bought 2 shares of the Citizens at $5.00 a share—my first stock purchase.

When I was 10, I wanted a bike desperately. Of course, I promised I would never leave the block. I got a second-hand girls bike for my birthday. On the first day I was gone—down to see the Falls. My Dad saw me from behind, pedaling like crazy, in freedom. I heard about that.

When I was 11, I asked a girl on a date to see a movie. I asked my Dad for a dollar to go to the movies. Boy, did I hear about that too. Dad gave me the dollar. I bought 2 children's tickets for 12¢ apiece. I never asked my Dad for another cent in my life, nor did I ever take another cent from him. I was going to make my own way. I was going on the adventure of life my way.

On the day I turned 12, I bought a paper route for $10.00. I borrowed the money to pay for the route from the seller to be paid from the earnings. My Dad demanded to know where I got the $10.00. Two weeks later, I threw the $10.00 in coins on the kitchen table with a loud "there's the $10.00." I regret to this day that I did it that way.

I was active in sports and played basketball and baseball. I particularly loved baseball and played through high school.

I always had a paper route, eventually buying two more routes. I sold the Niagara Falls Gazette for 5¢, earning 1.5¢ per paper. I had about 125 customers. I paid for all my personal expenses, all my clothes, coats and shoes since the day I turned 12. I saved about $1,000 in my savings account too.

I continued through the Niagara Falls School System playing sports, delivering papers, pumping gas, washing cars and doing various odd jobs through the 11th grade.

Many of my friends were athletes that played for Bishop Duffy Catholic High School. The guys were after me to switch to Bishop Duffy in my senior year. I had been doing well in the Falls school system, but I wanted to go to Catholic school. I approached my Dad. "No way are you going to do that" he said.

Jack at 17

We had several "discussions." Finally, Pop relented. He said "OK, but you pay the tuition." I said "OK." The tuition at Bishop Duffy was $50.00 a semester. I paid the tuition out of my paper route money.

I did well at Bishop Duffy, playing baseball and basketball (better at baseball).

About 2/3 through my senior year at Duffy, the family was having dinner. Pop looked up at me and said "I hear you want to go to college." I said "Yes, Dad—I was thinking about it." Dad simply said "OK, you figure out how to go." That was the only discussion we ever had about college.

While delivering my papers each day for 4 years, I passed the Niagara Falls Post Office each night. Outside the post office there was a recruiting poster with the picture of a sailor and a ship saying "Join the Navy and see the world!" I was always fascinated with that imaginative idea. I continued to read various adventure books about history and the Navy.

I was always fascinated by the stock market and would follow the market in the Niagara Falls Gazette and the Buffalo Evening News. I remember asking Mr. Vartanian at North Junior High School "what an option was?" He had no idea.

I had several great teachers at North Junior High School in 7th to 10th grades including Mr. Sdao, Miss Hayes and Mr. Overhauser in plain geometry. I still think the 10th grade Regent's exam in plain geometry gave me more anxious moments than any other exam. I won the Time Magazine Award in 10th grade on current events.

At Duffy, there was an advertisement on the bulletin board about taking a special examination for the Navy Reserve Officers Training Corps Scholarship Program.

I thought to take the exam. Upon studying, the program would pay tuition, $50.00 a month, books, travel and uniforms at any of the 52 colleges and universities throughout the country. First, one had to win the scholarship, then one had to be accepted by the chosen university, then one had to be accepted competitively into the unit of choice—and, of course, the physical. Then, every summer at sea, and, ultimately, a regular Navy commission into the fleet for 3 years, then 5 years to the ready reserve.

I took the exam, passed the interviews and got accepted into the program. There was only one problem—my Dad had to sign the papers as I was only 17. After much argument, Pop signed the papers to join the Navy if I won the scholarship.

I had also won a New York State Scholarship for $350 which could only be used in New York State. There was only one school in New York that had a Navy ROTC unit. That was Cornell.

So, I only applied to one school, Cornell, to attend the Arts and Sciences School. I knew I wanted to major in economics already. I paid the $15.00 application fee in cash, from my paper route money.

I remember writing my application in pen and ink promising that if they would give me a chance—and this was my only chance—I would make them proud. Cornell accepted me and I was one of about 20 freshman Navy scholarship winners in the class of 1958, starting as a freshman in September, 1954.

CORNELL AND THE NAVY

I started at Cornell in September, 1954. The Navy paid the $800.00 semi-annual tuition to the Arts and Sciences School. I remember thinking "How could anyone possibly pay that amount of money for tuition?" New York State paid $350.00 for my room by the beautiful World War I War Memorial dorm at the foot of the main campus hill. The Navy paid me $50.00 a month for expenses. My Mom said she and Dad would send me $50.00 a month for my board. The first week at school I got a note from my dear Mom with $5.00 in it. (I know it came from her grocery money). Mom said "we bought our first house in Lewiston and it had taken everything they had, including a note to the builder and a $2,500 down payment." I believe the purchase price was $16,500. My folks lived there at 449 Kenwood Drive in Lewiston for the rest of their lives.

So, I had to eat. I got a job waiting tables at one of the fraternities. I waited tables every meal for 4 years at Cornell. I think I did that at around 40 fraternities. I believe I was the world's worst waiter. The job supplied my food needs except for Sunday nights when no meals were served. The question was what to do for Sunday night dinner. I usually bought a pack of cigarettes for 35¢ instead of a hamburger at Williard Straight Hall. The cigarettes cut my appetite. For breakfast mostly I had a coke and a cigarette.

Studies went well particularly my history courses including Naval History. I have always loved history to this day. Ithaca had some severe weather, particularly in winter. My friends from New York City all complained. I told them "This is not so bad, you should have grown up in Western New York."

The USS Wisconsin

I pledged to Phi Kappa Psi fraternity, a fine bunch of guys. I enjoyed the fraternity life. Great parties, 18 year old drinking age—very liberal party policies—a lot of fun. I remember the first Fall Weekend—steak and lobster tail for dinner and scotch before. I enjoyed all three. I never had them before that Fall Weekend.

It was a good year. I found Cornell to be an outstanding school with a great faculty, great campus and very diversified.

I'm glad I went to the Arts School. I looked at a fraternity brother's Mechanical Engineering freshman course book. I don't think I would have lasted a week.

In the Navy ROTC Scholarship Program each scholarship student had to go for an eight-week summer course program. My first orders came in

May, 1955 to report aboard the Battleship USS Wisconsin for an eight-week summer cruise to visit Edinburgh and then Copenhagen. Wow! Forward is my motto! Adventure!

Before the ship left in July and school ended in June, I had an extra ten days. I needed some money so Dad got me a job working on the City of Niagara Falls yard gang at $1.35 an hour. OK, it was very educational. A physical exam was necessary before employment. I never forgot meeting several West Virginia ex-coal miners in the interview room. The men were desperate for work – they were worried they wouldn't make the exam because they had black lung disease. They were so sad when they left the exam room. I have never forgotten their faces.

So, I worked digging ditches with the Niagara Falls work crew. One man in particular I remembered. He snuck away every half hour or so behind a tree and drank from a hidden bottle of whiskey. He asked me to join him. I said "no".

Every Monday the work crew was short because many of the men did not report to work. On this particular Monday, the call then went out to put the "college kids" on the garbage trucks for the day. I learned more from that day than any other. The heat, the work, the smells, the sweat, the incredible hard work that many men do every day of their lives. I rode on the side of the truck to the dump. What a great breeze. I was hoping none of my friends would see me.

I have a tremendous amount of respect for all the men, and women who do so much physical work every day of their lives.

Time came to leave for the cruise. With my sea bag packed and good-byes said, off by bus to New York, then to West Orange, New Jersey, for an overnight stay with my great friend Mike Griffinger and his family. "Griff" and I met at our first Navy class. We became great friends and still are to this day. Mr. and Mrs. Griffinger drove us to Norfolk and we had dinner at the Norfolk Navy Yards Officers Club (we were allowed to do so as 3rd class midshipmen). The next morning, Mr. and Mrs. Griffinger drove us to the

Norfolk Pier where the battleship USS Wisconsin was moored, a sight I will never forget.

We drove to the pier. A thousand midshipmen from 52 colleges in uniform, all Navy scholarship students with their sea bags waiting to board the Wisconsin. It was the first time I ever saw a U.S. Navy "ship of the line" – the first time I had ever seen a battleship and the first time I had ever seen the ocean. The day was beautiful. The sights and sounds awesome. Adventure was in the air.

The 3rd class midshipmen did all the dirty jobs. Cleaning ship latrines, cleaning and washing the deck—all six acres of teak decks. We were loaders of 40 millimeter mounts during the firing exercises.

There were nine 16 inch guns on board the battleship. The shells were 6 feet high and weighed 2700 pounds. Six 150 lb. bags of black powder fired each gun. The shells were moved by a small train in the magazines. The Navy crew talked about each time the gun fired it was like shooting a "Cadillac" out the barrel ($4,500 in 1955).

In a firing exercise to see the explosions, feel the shudder of the ship and actually see the projectiles in flight was awesome. A U.S. battleship in fighting mode is a sight to see.

Seeing these sights and others on the trip was something I never forgot. To think that we could use these weapons against other human beings essentially made me a pacifist. I believe that military power should be used as a last resort. I believe in a strong military. I do think that all U.S. citizens should give some of their time in service to their country. The problem with an all-volunteer force is that it is so good that politicians are enticed to over-use the armed forces for short term political purposes.

We stopped in Edinburgh for a week. The first time a major U.S. battleship had docked since World War II, into the Firth of Forth and under the bridge. What a reception! Scotland was a beautiful country with beautiful people. We loved the week. We then sailed through the Straits of Dover to Copenhagen which was a great city. I loved the people. Then, back to sea. A great education and great learning experience. Experience of a battleship of the line. Unforgettable. Then back to Ithaca and sophomore year. At Cornell, in those days, one needed to be proficient in a foreign language by the end of sophomore year or "bye-bye".

Sophomore year caused a "sophomore slump." I was the world's worst French student. Although I passed my proficiency exam, but nonetheless went on scholastic probation. I bought a 1949 Ford V8 car with 83,000 miles on it and lots of rust, for $150.00. I could drive back and forth to Lewiston instead of hitchhiking. The car had dual exhausts and a very loud straight thru exhaust. The V8 engine ran great. I drove it for 50,000 miles, put in a quart of oil every couple of months and never gave the car any service. The engine still ran when I scrapped it in May, 1958. The car was named the "Green Goose". I floored it every time I ever ran it.

We made many trips to Wells College and I used the car for my sandwich business in the evenings. I would make sandwiches in the afternoon, then take them around to the fraternities in the evening. I would make some money, but it took me 3 or 4 hours. So much for my study habits. We made a convertible out of the "Green Goose" on Fall Weekend, 1958 by chopping the top off with an ax. What a party!

So I was on probation the end of my sophomore year. Then off to military training for the summer. The first month we were assigned to marine training in Little Creek, Virginia. Drilling, map reading and small arms training in case we wanted to become marine officers. We went to sea and made an amphibious landing, I believe somewhere in North Carolina. We were three days on a troop ship then a landing with regular marines. I carried a bazooka and shells through a jungle and swamp for a number of miles through the morning.

When we finished, I went to take a swig of water from my canteen and I really caught hell from a Mississippi marine 2nd Lieutenant. In no uncertain language, he told me "no water unless I say so." Not quite that language.

We finished and went to the marine food line for lunch. I never forgot the food in the line—watermelon, chicken, fresh tomatoes, oranges, etc. Never in my life had I seen such food as was on that line.

Now across a few hundred yards to bleachers set up on what looked like a regular football field. We all sat in the bleachers. Then a Marine Corps Sergeant said "and now gentlemen you will see a demonstration of Marine Corps firepower!"

Marine howitzers opened up from miles away. Shell after shell pounded up from one end of the field to the other. The bombardment lasted 2 or 3 minutes right in front of our eyes. The field was walked by the artillery shells every five yards from one end to the other.

The noise and explosions were unbelievable. The sulphuric gas and smells and sounds of the shells was almost unbearable. At the end of the demonstration there was absolute silence. I never had seen or heard anything like it in my life. I didn't think then that I wanted to be a marine officer as an option.

Then a flight to Corpus Christi, Texas, and training with the Navy Air Training Command. We flew seaplanes and also the Navy two-seater jet trainers, the TV2. I enjoyed the jet training and thought I might want to be a carrier pilot.

One had to pass a swimming test to become an officer. 900 midshipmen jumped in the pool in Corpus Christi. I think we had to swim six or eight lengths. I was the last one out of the pool. I only made it by paddling on my back, floating and every other method of propulsion through the water. The entire class of midshipmen cheered me on as I was the last one out of the pool by a long shot.

Cornell for junior year in the Fall. I had to get off probation or I would be out of Cornell and lose my chance. I worked hard and got off probation.

I majored in economics and loved the courses. The only professor I was close to was Professor Alfred Kahn. He had graduated from Columbia at 19 and was absolutely brilliant. He would teach a course without a note.

He eventually became head of the Public Service Commission, then under President Carter, head of the Civil Aeronautics Board. He was the father of airline deregulation.

I corresponded with him occasionally and saw him and had a great chat with him at my 50th Alumni Reunion. He always had time for this C student (maybe B in his course).

Towards the end of my junior year, friends thought I should run for Student Council since I knew so many people—so I ran for Senior Class President and won. My motto was "bigger and better." How could I lose? I ran for President of Phi Kappa Psi and got beat.

Jack ready to fly off
FDR-1957

Off to the Navy again in the summer of 1957. The assignment was to the U.S. Aircraft carrier Franklin D. Roosevelt. Only twelve First Class Midshipmen were assigned to the FDR to cruise with the 6th Fleet in the Mediterranean.

In the first several weeks, we were assigned to the Engineering Department. I was assigned to follow a very fine young Lt. JG. I spent the day with him every day. On about the tenth day, I was to meet him after lunch at 1300 hours. I was a little late, playing poker. About 1308, a steam wheel went off its moorings and cut a steam line. The ship went dead in the water. Six men were killed and many injured by the violent steam rupture. I never saw that Lt. JG again.

We went to the 6th Fleet Operations to France. Our first stop was to Cannes on the Riviera. The French girls all came out in their bikinis on their little paddle wheel boats to greet the ship. What an introduction to France! We viewed a lot of air operations including many night time operations. They were a miracle to see.

Planes coming in at high speeds, one after another, being stopped by a cable wire and hook on the plane. The noise and teamwork was incredible. I did a take-off and landing in an AD Skyraider. I still have the picture. Some unforgettable experience. I wasn't sure I still wanted to become a Navy pilot.

We flew back from Barcelona. Griff and I went out for a big night. Lots of Spanish wine, dancing and guitar playing. We did just make the plane on our way back for senior year. It was September, 1957.

Jack taking off in A.D. Skyraider
USS Franklin Roosevelt 1957

We were ready to go. Senior year came and went. There were battles with the Cornell Administration over apartment rules and student social policy. President Dean Malotte was hung in effigy. By the end of May, 1958, the class was ready to go into the world.

We were commissioned upon graduation. My selection was to go into the "Black Shoe" Navy and in June I was ordered to the U.S. destroyer ship the USS Kenneth D. Bailey (DDR 713) stationed at Newport, Rhode Island. The ship was named for a marine Major killed at Guadalcanal in the early part of World War II.

First, a three-week assignment to Little Creek, Virginia, for communications training. Griff and I were roommates at Little Creek. We had been together on the Wisconsin, with the Marines, on the FDR and now we were assigned to the same destroyer squadron (Desron 8). He was assigned to the USS Goodrich (DDR 831).

After about 10 days at Little Creek, I was called down by the commanding officer and told to pack my bags and the Bailey was coming down from Newport to Norfolk to pick me up. "Be on the pier and ready to go at 1800 hours." The Bailey came in at 1800, I saluted, and reported on board. The ship backed out and headed immediately to Lebanon (July, 1958).

The captain informed me immediately that from that moment I was in charge of all communications as Communications Officer and, by the way, I was also Communications Officer for Desron 8 as the Desron 8 Squadron Commander was based on the Bailey.

I spent a long 9 months with the 6th Fleet. We went fully operational and stayed at sea 42 days while taking part in the marine invasion of Beirut in August of 1958. The marines invaded Beirut under President Eisenhower's orders.

I was in Beirut several times. It was difficult. There were so many political factions. Each time one walked down a different street you could feel the gun sights in your back, each time by a different faction.

The USS Kenneth D. Bailey

We visited many of the Mediterranean ports including Athens, Rhodes, Cannes, Monte Carlo, Naples and more.

Unfortunately, we had a very severe collision at sea in January, 1958. The Bailey was hit outside of Gibraltar by a USMTS supply ship, the USS Haiti Victory. The Victory had a cement reinforced bow which sliced through the starboard side of the Bailey like butter.

I had been on the bridge of the Bailey early as I was officer of the deck getting underway from Gibraltar. I was very glad to have been relieved after about an hour because the Gibraltar Strait traffic was very heavy and we were running high speed destroyer screens looking for submarines waiting for the two main aircraft carriers to follow us out and "go home."

I went to the Officers wardroom (just below the bridge) for a cup of coffee sitting with Lt. Pete Petit, the Commodore's Chief of Staff. All of a sudden we were tossed about hard. I thought we had run aground. Then an alarm went off. I hadn't heard that alarm before. Pete said "That's the collision alarm."

The ship had stopped and started to list. I ran up to the bridge, and saw Captain Philabauer and said "What happened?" All he said was "shit!"

I ran over the bridge to the starboard side and saw a huge ship stuck in the starboard side. I ran aft and the crew was pulling men from the water. The bow had entered into the 2nd Division Compartment, my division.

Unfortunately, we lost able seaman Kelley that day, one of my men. I pray for him every day.

It was a truly lucky day for the rest of us. The bow missed our after depth charges by only a couple of feet and entered through the 2nd Division Compartment, opening up the after magazine and going to the starboard shaft.

The USS Kenneth D. Bailey

The ship was immobile and listing heavily to starboard. We were towed into the Spanish shipyard in Gibraltar and proceeded to have a patch put on the starboard side. The hole was gigantic. My remembrance was around 20 feet by 20 feet. The starboard drive shaft was out of commission. So, we only had one screw for propulsion. After 6 weeks in Gibraltar to patch the side, our orders were to go to the Boston Naval Shipyard for repairs.

We had a very rough Atlantic crossing in March of 1959 coming back on one screw through the wintry Atlantic. We were accompanied by another Navy ship in case we got into trouble. I remember looking up once at a gigantic wave coming over the bridge. I didn't know if we would make it.

We spent 3 months in the Boston Navy Shipyard fixing the damaged ship.

I finally saw my parents after a year and the first thing Dad said was "What happened to you?" I said "Dad, it's a long story." I had lost 20 pounds. A little leave then back to the Bailey. The ship left Boston for Newport home base. Captain Philabauer was relieved after the court of inquiry.

By that time I was made Gunnery Officer in Command of all the ships armaments (5" 38 main guns, 3" 50 antiaircraft batteries, depth charges, anti-submarine torpedoes and antisubmarine equipment, about 100 men and 3 other officers. I was 24.

The ship was ordered to Mayport, Florida as a new home base. We spent some time there – then to the 2nd Fleet in Guantanamo Bay, Cuba for training. We were also looking for gun-runners into Central and South

America. We left Guantanamo and headed for another tour to the 6th Fleet. Lots of sea duty and travel through the Mediterranean.

I decided not to stay in the Navy but I didn't know what I was going to do.

We were headed to Naples, Italy. When we docked the new captain, Captain Wiegard said to me "JB, I'm going to give you a reward. Take a bus load of sailors to Rome for 3 days. You'll be in charge – enjoy yourselves." So I took a busload of sailors from Naples to Rome for 3 days.

Jack 1960

I lined up the men in Rome as they got off the bus and said "Gentlemen, enjoy yourselves. Don't get into trouble. I'll be here at this "pension" in 3 days and the bus will leave immediately at 0800 hours."

Three days later all 33 sailors showed up and we went home to the ship. The sailors on the Bailey were so great in so many ways. I will always be proud of what they did and how they did it. All Americans should be proud of their Navy men.

I went to Frankfurt and flew home on a MSTS 707 just after it came into service. I was mustered out in late May 1961 in Philadelphia. I took the bus home to Lewiston, New York. I had saved $300 in mustering out pay and had bought an old 1954 Austin Healey Roadster. I had a five-year reserve commitment, too. I made $212.50 a month as an Ensign and $312.50 as a Lieutenant Junior Grade. I was 25 with no college debt.

NEW YORK AND WALL STREET – THE START

I came out of the Navy in late May, 1961. I had a dear friend in New York from college days, Bill Miller. Bill was a fraternity brother and a real genuine great character.

I came to New York to visit Bill and his new wife Sandy. I stayed on Bill's front couch in Brooklyn Heights while I interviewed for a job. Bill had a friend who was a U.S. Treasury bond broker. I ended up being hired by the U.S. Government Securities dealer CF Childs and Company as a "board boy." A "board boy" stood at a blackboard and changed chalk securities prices with an eraser after having been called "boy – change the price on the 2.5% of '72." I had 100 men under me on the Bailey and I started as a "board boy" at CF Childs. It was a start at $400 a month.

I stayed with Sandy and Bill for 6 months on that couch. They were magnificent in their generosity and kindness.

I got my first apartment in New York, a one bedroom, at 235 Adams Street in Brooklyn Heights. An old classmate, Bill Rau was my roommate. We split the $129.00 a month rent.

We had no furniture. A trader at CF Childs had been successful and was selling his old furniture from his apartment. He said he would take $700 for it and he thought it was sold and would be picked up on Saturday morning, but I could come and look at it. I went to his apartment about 1:00 o'clock and the furniture was still there. He said "I guess the other guy didn't show up." I said "Dutch (Dutch Ostema was his name) I'll tell you what I will do. I'll pay you $25.00 in cash for all of it and $25.00 a month for three months and I'll have it out of here by this afternoon." "Sold to you" he shouted. I took it and kept my side of the deal. We used the furniture at my bachelor apartment.

Most of the guys on Wall Street were old timers. Many in the government bond community were deferred from World War II because their jobs were labeled so important in the financing of the war. Very few young people came to Wall Street from the 1930's to the 50's. CF Childs was trying to bring some young people into the business to grow. As I said, "It was a start." Once I got started, I knew I would find my way.

As I started to understand the business, I picked up a phone and started cold calling some institutions about government and corporate bonds. Within 9 months, I was the number one producing corporate bond salesman in the firm and made assistant vice-president. My pay went to $7,500 a year plus commissions.

I came to the attention of a young tax-free bond trader and salesman by the name of A.P. Kelley (Al). He liked me and told me he was going to start his own municipal bond firm. After a while, he made me an offer to be his number two as executive vice-president in his new firm, A.P. Kelley and Company. I said, "Al, I have no capital." He said "That's ok. I have $25,000 and I have a silent partner with $75,000. If you come with me as my number two, I will give you 1/3 of the company in 3 years, and I will teach you the municipal bond business."

A few days earlier, I had called the Navy Department in Washington. I said "If you'll give me the job as Chief of Staff for the Admiral of the 7th Fleet in Hong Kong, I'll come back to the Navy (I was a full lieutenant in the reserves then). The Navy called me back the next day and said "Come on back, the job is yours." I went that afternoon to the Statue of Liberty and smoked a big cigar. I thought for a few minutes, to Hong Kong or start a new company? I threw the cigar down and said "I'll start the company." I called the Navy Department the next day and said I wasn't coming back in.

Al and I opened A.P. Kelley and Company May 31, 1962 with offices at 40 Exchange Place, New York, N.Y. On June 1, 1962, Al borrowed $10,000,000 from the Franklin Bank and the Grace Bank to fund our trading positions.

Ingrid 1963

We stayed at 100x leverage or more for approximately 5 years during a terrible bear bond market, eventually merging with a medium sized New York Stock Exchange firm Schweickert and Co. to become Schweickert's Institutional Bond Department. We opened A.P. Kelley and Co. on May 31, 1962. I had been on Wall Street all of 111/2 months.

We got the company off the ground working 7 days a week, 20 hours a day. I was learning trading and selling and we were making a name for ourselves in the municipal trading and underwriting community.

I had not gone out since the company started but thought I would make New Year's Eve 1962 my first big night out. A friend had invited me to a party.

I bought a new custom-made suit at Wanamaker's and planned a big night out.

My friend's apartment was in Queens, out by Idlewild Airport. I thought I might meet some Swedish stewardesses. I had never been to a party in Queens, but there was always a first time. I arrived at the party in my new suit at about 9:45 p.m. carrying a bottle of scotch. The party was going on big time. It was a riot. A lot of noise and music.

I knocked on the door, was invited in and then...the door opened, and as I walked in the party was going on big time. As I turned my head to review the scene, there was a beautiful blonde with upswept hair about 12 feet to my right surrounded by 3 or 4 fellows. As I came in she turned towards me and our eyes met for a second. I said "My God—what is that?" She was the most beautiful woman that I had ever seen.

I eventually went over to say hello and introduced myself. "What is your name, I asked." "Ingrid," she said, "it's my first party here in America."

Ingrid's Story

Ingrid's story was incredible too. She was born in Efferen, Germany on October 25, 1940 as Ingrid Rosa Schneider.

Her home was destroyed in the allied bombings of Cologne, so she grew up in the tiny German farm community of Hermulheim.

Ingrid with her younger brother and sister
Germany 1944

Ingrid, her mother, brother and sister, as refugees, lived in one room in a farmhouse on a working farm. There was no indoor plumbing and very little food. Ingrid's mom collected leftover potatoes from the field after harvest, then made gravy with one piece of bacon. Ingrid had only one doll in her life, which she loved. Her mother would make a new dress for the doll out of an old army blanket at Christmas. Ingrid attended a one-room schoolhouse and remembered rolling a tire down a hill with a stick for fun.

Ingrid suffered terribly from diphtheria and tuberculosis of her lungs and bones. She was sent to the North Sea in the hope that the salt air would help to cure her – then to a German sanitarium. Her father rushed back from the eastern front to see her as she was close to death. Miraculously she recovered.

Ingrid's father had been drafted into the German Army at the age of 38 and served as a medic. He was captured by the Russians at the historic 1944 battle of Stalingrad. He spent 8 years in a Russian prison camp in the Gulag in Siberia. He returned to Germany in 1952. He had to sell clothing door-to-door to make a living until he got cleared by intelligence to receive his old job back at an insurance company in Cologne. He was one of only 7,000 men that returned from the Stalingrad battle out of a German Army of 700,000 men.

Ingrid and her mom were on a train that was attacked by allied planes in 1944. The family was separated during the attack and a German soldier spent three days finding the family members and making sure they were safe. He was three days late reporting back to the Russian eastern front and was executed by firing squad for desertion.

I remembered seeing a Christmas card from the soldier's family in Ingrid's affects. There was a Christmas card to Ingrid's dad too, with a lock of her blond hair.

The family eventually moved back to Cologne and rebuilt their house on the same land, as Cologne was rebuilt.

Ingrid became an expert in German Porcelain and antique porcelain, and got a job in a shop near the Cologne Cathedral that catered to foreign tourists. She met some Americans and loved their freedom and openness.

She thought she might like to go to America. She told her family and they all laughed at her. She went to the German Embassy in Cologne to find out the requirements. They told her there was a need for children's nurses in America and if she qualified as a nurse, possibly she could get a position for a year or two. So, Ingrid went to a hospital in Cologne and trained as a children's nurse to qualify.

The family still laughed, but not after she received a job offer from a Westchester family. On the day she turned 21, her father drove her to Rotterdam to say "goodbye." She never saw her mother again after that day.

Ingrid stayed with the family in Westchester for about 9 months as an "Au Pair" taking care of five children. She decided to leave her job, having saved $50 and proceeded to Grand Central Station in New York. Alone, knowing no one, no friends, and no job. She entered Grand Central Station with three phone numbers of hostels in New York where single European girls could safely stay. The first two numbers she called had no availability. She connected on the third number and went down to Greenwich Village. The next day she applied to Tiffany's and received a job offer for $75.00 a week. She then accepted a job at Ginori at 5th Avenue and 48th Street for $85.00 a week where she could work in the shop and do the windows too.

She survived on Campbell's Soup and beans and treated herself to one good meal a week. She learned English by watching television.

She met a Russian girl at Ginori's, who was invited by a friend to a New Year's Eve party out by Idlewild Airport. Ingrid said she couldn't go because she didn't have an escort. The Russian girl said "This is America – you don't need an escort." Ingrid went to that New Year's Eve party, December 31, 1962.

The rest is history, and part of our "Great American Love Story." Wow! Thanks to everyone for being part of this American miracle.

THE NEW LIFE

*I*ngrid and I talked on that New Year's Eve. We had a great time even though she was just learning English.

We left the party in Queens together as I told her there was another party in Brooklyn Heights where I had my apartment. Some Cornell friends were raising hell. We went to that party and had a lot of fun. Everything was new for Ingrid. Ingrid stayed with my friends and we went to a milk punch party in Brooklyn Heights at the home of my great old friend, David Guest on New Year's Day.

We saw each other often starting in January, 1963. Unfortunately, Ingrid's Mom died early in 1963 and Ingrid was heartbroken. She didn't find out about the death until the day of the funeral and couldn't make it back. It was heartbreaking for Ingrid not to make it back. She thought she probably would have to go back to Germany and take care of her younger sister and brother and her Dad as she was the oldest.

After several months, Ingrid invited me back to her Weehawken apartment for dinner. I accepted. What a dinner it was. I had never been to Weehawken before or since. Ingrid bought a small bottle of scotch, poured me a drink and served a most beautiful dinner.

The table was perfect – flowers, setting, and music. It was a wow! Then dessert – a most beautiful cake with strawberries on top, all perfectly placed.

I said "You certainly have some baker that you used to make such a beautiful cake." She looked at me with her beautiful green eyes and said "No—I baked that cake..."

At the end of the evening, all I could think of was Ingrid.

We continued to date. One Sunday, I said "I'm going to shop for a new car. Would you like to come?" I had to replace my old 1954 Austin Healey Roadster.

Ingrid and Jack Marry July 18, 1963
St. Peters Church, Lewiston, NY

Someone had thrown a brick through the windshield in Brooklyn Heights, then had stolen the replacement. We went to the Triumph dealer. I was thinking about a Triumph 3 or 4. I had always wanted an XKE though. We went to the XKE dealer too.

As the spring went on, we fell in love. I asked Ingrid to marry me in the late spring of 1963. We were very happy. I said "I was a risk taker and I wasn't sure where business would take me and I wasn't sure I would be successful."

She said in her beautiful accent, "I don't care what happens. As long as you love me, I will be happy in one room with just an electric bulb." That was enough for me. I had saved $2,000 and had two new suits.

We couldn't make it back to Germany for the wedding so we decided to marry in July, 1963 in Lewiston, New York, my home. My family was excited. We got married July 17, 1963 at St. Peters Church in Lewiston, New York.

I told Ingrid to get a wedding dress. She bought a beautiful one at Macy's in Herald Square for $50.00. We had the reception at my folks' home in Lewiston. The family pitched in.

Drinks were served, the food was good and plentiful and fun was had by all. The reception cost me $300.00.

I had leased a red XKE in the interim and we had a lot of fun with that. We used to go to the car races in Bridgehampton with the top down on the Long Island Expressway with Ingrid in her polka dot bikini. Wow! As always, she stopped the traffic.

After our wedding, we honeymooned in Nassau. Ingrid loved it. She had never seen a palm tree before. We had a wonderful time. I smoked my last cigarette in a limo to the hotel—threw the butt out the window and never had another.

Ingrid became pregnant with our first son John in 1964. We were living in my old bachelor pad in Brooklyn Heights.

Ingrid, Mom Kelly and Jack
Lewiston home 1980

I was working hard but I needed to make some money to buy a house. I had an old friend who was an analyst on Wall Street. He told me about a company he knew of that made steam shovels called Bucyrus Erie. He said they might make a couple or more shovels in the next few years. So I bought 500 shares of Bucyrus Erie at $8,000 total. I had saved $4,000, every cent I had in the world. I borrowed 50% of the purchase price on margin. It was every cent I could beg or borrow. I walked across the Brooklyn Bridge that night because I didn't have fifteen cents for the subway. I never told Ingrid.

A year later, I sold the 500 shares of Bucyrus Erie at 36 and made a profit of $10,000. I paid $2,000 in capital gains taxes and bought a beautiful Tudor home in Ridgewood, New Jersey for $32,000. I made the buying bid the night we bombed Hanoi in Vietnam.

We rented a U-Haul and drove our stuff from the apartment in the U-Haul down the Westside Highway. We moved in with help from our dear old friends David and Naomi Guest. Ingrid, seven months pregnant, was bouncing along the Westside Highway ready for our new home.

John and Rob
Normandy Beach 1969

We loved our Ridgewood house. It was a beautiful Tudor. John was born in January 1965 at Cornell Hospital in New York. We picked him up in a snowstorm and put him on the floor of the XKE, a two-seater. We drove him around like that for 3 years, no seat belt. Ingrid didn't drive so we would go shopping on Saturday morning with John on the floor and bags of groceries all over the open car.

Ingrid became pregnant with our son Rob so we needed a new car. I traded the perfect red XKE for a 1967 Ford Fairlane convertible. I said at the time "This will be the worst trade I will ever make in my life". It was the worst trade I ever made. I saw an absolute matching red XKE in Gladstone last week for $175,000.

I commuted from Ridgewood for 4 years. A.P. Kelley was struggling. We had a terrible bond market from 1963 to 1967 with bond prices going down about 40%. We were always under a lot of pressure. Al Kelley was a real character. We had a black tie New Year's Eve dinner party for our friends celebrating our meeting and new life.

Al was at the party and extolling one of my marine friends on his abilities as a Marine officer and pilot. I saw my friend the next day (an ex-Marine Captain) and he told me how fascinated he was by Al's stories as a Marine flying officer. Al had a vivid imagination and, of course, he was never a Marine officer, or pilot.

Ingrid and I bought a beautiful oceanfront beach house in Normandy Beach, New Jersey for $52,000. We both loved the ocean. We rented the house for 1⁄2 seasons and gave the money to my parents so they could retire. Ingrid did everything.

Al merged A.P. Kelley with Schweickert and Company in 1968. A.P. Kelley became the institutional arm of Schweickert. Al and I broke up and I became the Tax Free Institutional Sales Manager for Thomson McKinnon, a medium-sized New York Stock Exchange firm.

Schweickert was a partnership and went under in the 1968 market crash. CF Childs and Co. disappeared after the crash of 1962-63 as well as A.P. Kelley in 1968. Al went down with the Schweickert crash and went to Little Rock to start again.

I saw him one more time at lunch in Fraunces Tavern in 1969. He asked me what I liked in the market. I told him silver at $1.39 an ounce. It had just gone to a free market. Al came to New York a few months later to Sloan Kettering for cancer treatment. He died shortly thereafter at 41. I ran and built Thomson McKinnon's Institutional Tax Free Bond sales force from 1968 to 1974.

After the crash of '68, few jobs were available on "the street" for bankers of any sort. In stocks the favorite 50 stocks were bid up to 50 times earnings. It didn't make any difference what you paid for a company as long as you got the growth. I thought the notion was ridiculous and went to all cash in 1972. I saw the crash of 1973-74 coming and was prepared.

I wanted to move from Ridgewood as John and Robert were growing and I was thinking about heading west, getting some land, perhaps a small farm so John and Rob could learn some things by doing some hard physical work.

Ingrid and I bought a beautiful house on 5+ acres in Tewksbury Township and added another 61/2 acres to it next door for cash at the bottom of the market. At one time I owned three houses. The Ridgewood house was sold three times before it closed. A French banker bought it having given me a $100 credit prior to closing. The French Bank would give him a mortgage he said.

At the bottom of the 1973-74 market there were 500 stocks selling at 5 times earnings. The Arab oil boycott was on. There was no money for mortgages. Gasoline was very scarce and rarely available.

We had one 1973 Camaro. Ingrid drove me to the Gladstone train and picked me up at night. Tremendous country snow storms came – for six weeks we had to bring up our groceries by sled as we could not get up our driveway.

Thomson made it through this difficult market and I built a good business by cold calling banks and insurance companies and eventually running many institutional tax free bond portfolios.

Rob and John started at the local Tewksbury schools and eventually both went to Delbarton School, a Benedictine school in Morristown. Both boys were "lifers" starting in 7th grade. John graduated in 1983 and Rob in 1986.

Ingrid ran the farm taking responsibility for everything. We had sheep, goats, miniature horses, a tennis court, and the works. Ingrid also kept up our shore house in Normandy Beach. In the summer she did everything at both houses. I was a sole proprietor in the business at Thomson for all those years.

I've only taken one two-week vacation. That was in 1971. I had a great month – so we spent one week with the boys and my parents in Vermont skiing and then a week to ourselves in Grenada.

In 1968, I went to Germany to meet Ingrid's Dad. Ingrid was pregnant with Rob but preceded me by a week with John. I got off the plane, handed my father-in-law a box of cigars and a bottle of scotch saying "Hi Poppa, I'm Jack."

We got along very well. Poppa came to visit us in Ridgewood and at the New Jersey Shore. We had a great relationship. He had been a medic in the German Army, having been drafted at 38 into the Army. He was captured at the Battle of Stalingrad, spent 8 years in the Gulag in Siberia and was one of only 7,000 out of an army of 700,000 that returned from Russia in 1952. He knew how much Ingrid and I loved each other.

We consistently traveled in the 70's and 80's with Thomson. Sometimes we took trips with John and Robert to Europe, visiting Germany, Switzerland, France and Ireland. When the boys were 10 and 7, they came down by train by themselves from Cologne to Lausanne for a few days—then through France to Paris and home.

Thomson was a private company and the firm's major producers and senior executives would plan trips together. At different times, we went to France, Greece, Turkey, Kenya, Rio, Hawaii and Australia among others.

Ingrid's father in Germany, 1967

Thomson Management made a major mistake and expanded their real estate holdings just prior to the crash of 1987. We moved into a new office building on August 25, 1987. The market went down 20% in the September 12, 1987 crash and the firm was forced to sell to Prudential Securities. The firm was owned by the 5000 employees in an Employee Stock Ownership Plan (ESOP). The common stock equity was wiped out so for the most part the employees received nothing for their many years of hard work. My equity position was wiped out along with everyone else. We all did not have a tax loss as the IRS ruled that we had never received the equity, the ESOP did not vest "therefore, no equity received, no loss."

Rob, Jack and John – Windsong Farm 2015

Thomson was merged into Prudential Securities in 1988. Our new office was on the 48th floor at One Liberty Plaza right across from the World Trade Center North Tower.

My son John had joined me in business in August 1987, six weeks before the crash in September 1987. He experienced the crash that day. He turned to me and said "What are you going to do?" I said "not a god-dammed thing—wait until it settles out." What a day. Impossible to get an execution of a trade.

After John and I joined Prudential, Rob Kelly said he would like to join us if possible. I was joyful that Rob wanted to come on board. The Kelly Group was started and on the move! We decided in 1990 to leave the institutional bond business and concentrate on money management for families. We have worked hard together for almost 35 years now and have built a great family business together.

John and Rob have been incredibly fine sons, everything that a man could want. They were raised to be independent. They have been great partners in the business and have become great husbands and fathers. They love their families and their country and are working hard every day with faith, spirit and love to build their own legacies.

In 1993, we experienced the massive truck bombing explosion at the World Trade Center. Our building shook so hard that I thought a gigantic bomb had gone off. I believe six people died and the damage was great.

We were together too, on the morning of September 11, 2001, on the 48th floor of One Liberty Plaza directly across from the North Tower on Hudson Street.

I heard the first attacking plane about 5 seconds before it flew directly over our heads and flew directly into the North Tower. I knew the plane or missile (I thought it might have been a missile) was going way too fast for the airspace. The engines were going at maximum revolutions per minute. I calculated about 430-440 MPH as I knew from my Navy experience how jet engines sounded at maximum RPM. I had also been a Navy air controller so I had experience controlling Navy jet fighters.

The plane passed above our head with a ferocious roar and crashed in front of our eyes into the North Tower. We saw it go through and out the West side of the building.

The air was full of paper and flames were starting to spew out. It looked like a Steven Spielberg movie – except it was real.

Many employees hovered in our office trying to figure out what to do and came into our office because of the view. Eventually after the 2nd plane hit the South Tower, I remember yelling "It's a terrorist attack" – and walking with everyone down the 48 floors to the street. John, Rob, my nephew Kevin Hogan, my friend John Spohler and his client all down into the street. I ran to the corner, took one last look at the Towers and came back to our group telling everyone "they're coming down—let's get out of here."

We locked arms and stayed together moving up Broadway through the mayhem to City Hall then North on Hudson Street towards Greenwich Village, to Rob's apartment. I said "they won't attack there." About halfway up Hudson Street, I looked back and saw the first Tower go down. I said "don't look back, keep going."

We got to Rob's apartment around 9:25 a.m., turned the TV on and both towers were gone. I had made a quick phone call to Ingrid seconds after the first plane hit saying "something big was going on, but we were ok" but got cut off after a couple of seconds.

The day was horrible in every way. One thing I will always remember every day of my life was seeing the first fire truck responding to the first attack. Every day I see those brave men getting out of their truck, putting on their equipment as they do, methodically, then slowly lining up and moving out in single file slowly to their certain death as they looked ahead to the scene. I believe about 300 firefighters died that day. God bless their souls. The tears of sadness fall on this paper as I write this, June 30, 2021, almost 20 years later.

We are pulling out of Afghanistan in a couple of weeks. It looks to me like another disaster is coming.

We moved uptown to the Chrysler Building for three months before returning downtown.

The Kelly Group moved to Legg Mason at 1 Chase Manhattan Plaza in 2001. Legg was a good home and our business grew well, growing one family at a time. The Kelly Group was building a great wealth management business. Together when we left Prudential we were managing and advising about $165,000,000; today it is over $2 billion dollars. Eventually Legg Mason was merged into Smith Barney. We went to Smith Barney on the merger and continued to build the business.

John and Rob got married and started to build their families with their beautiful wives Jennifer and Vidhya. John has three beautiful girls Emma, Avery and Brigid and lives in Chatham, New Jersey. Rob has one girl Jaya and twin boys Lekh and Shail. They live in Union Square in Manhattan.

We moved our business to JPMorgan Securities (previously Bear Stearns) in March of 2009 exactly at the 2009 market bottom to the day. Bear Stearns had been taken over by JPMorgan earlier that year and we knew the firm would be stable. We had previously turned down an employment offer from Bear Stearns several years before. I looked at their balance sheet and didn't like it.

We left Smith Barney after they were going to be taken over by Morgan Stanley. We didn't like the long contract offered.

We all worked hard through the 90's and 2000's continuing to build the business and invest for ourselves. John, Rob and I have been equal partners these many years and have continuously built the business. I am proud that we have built together a premiere intergenerational wealth management business that has had a real positive impact on the families that we serve. We pride ourselves in working with and educating 2nd and 3rd generation members of our clients' families.

Ingrid and I have had a very joyful life experience together. We have now been married 54 joyful years. What a wonderful American adventure it has been. We have lived on our small farm outside of Pottersville, New Jersey, about 30 miles west of New York, about 1 1/2 miles from President Trump's place in Bedminster. We moved to the country in 1973 and have always loved it. I commute from Far Hills, New Jersey, usually by train.

Ingrid has always run our homes in a magnificent way. She loves her gardens, her wildflowers, her animals and the beautiful peace that surrounds us at Windsong.

Ingrid and Jack at a costume party

The name Windsong came from my venture selling Windsong perfume on the Cornell Campus in 1957. I remember making $600 in November 1957 selling Windsong perfume to the fraternity brothers and friends as Christmas gifts for their mothers and girlfriends. Always the entrepreneur!

Ours has been a wonderful and fruitful life. We have worked hard enjoying the freedom and joy of America. We started with almost nothing in material wealth and have used the opportunity to have a great life working hard and happily.

We are now 81 and 77 respectively. We still get up at 4:30 a.m. Ingrid makes breakfast every day and we enjoy it together at 5 before I catch the 6:03 a.m. train from Far Hills to Penn Station, then two subways to our office at JPMorgan Securities at 277 Park Avenue.

We love our home at Windsong and look forward to coming back at night for a lovely dinner together. We always had dinner together with John and Rob when they were growing up.

We wanted to write this story together because we have had such a happy and fruitful life together.

Our two sons, John and Rob, have been wonderful sons and we have loved them with all our hearts. We are fortunate to have two great daughters-in-law, Jennifer and Vidhya with six beautiful grandchildren, Emma, Avery, and Brigid Kelly in John's family and Jaya, Lekh and Shail with Rob and Vidhya.

Ingrid and I are survivors. We have lived through the depression, World War II, the Korean War, the market crash of 1962, the crash of 1968, the crash of 1973-74, the crash of 1979-80, the crash of 1987, the internet crash of 2001, the crash of 2008-09 and the continuing turmoil of today's world with its ever increasing speed to change.

We have only taken one two-week vacation and that was in 1971.

I last picked up a pen almost 3 years ago. Ingrid will be 80 in October and I'm looking forward to my 84th in June. Today is April 2, 2020. I'm in quarantine at Windsong with Ingrid for the Coronavirus. Rob is at 277 Park Avenue, the only person on the entire floor. Everyone else has been sent home. Rob works from his home on Union Square too. Almost everything in New York is closed. No shows, no crowds in Times Square and few businesses open. There are many, many new cases and deaths every day. John is in Chatham and our support staff is scattered from Michigan to Pennsylvania.

Ingrid and Jack with the grandchildren

I became ill with a virus and spent 49 days in Morristown Memorial Hospital and Sloan Kettering in New York. After 49 days, the Sloan Kettering doctors came in and said "you're improving, you're getting better, you can go home." What a gift. I thought I couldn't wait to get home. Thirty days without a shower at Sloan Kettering. Two weeks in intensive care! They thought I had been attacked by a virus but were never sure. They called me "the miracle man."

I got home, and two weeks later, my dearest Ingrid was admitted to Morristown Memorial for quintuple bypass heart surgery. She is recovering well. We are both so thankful to all the dedicated nurses and doctors that have been so great to us during those tough months in 2019.

Now the entire country is suffering from coronavirus and what suffering it is. Our entire country is mostly shut down. The shutdown is affecting every person and every family. The personal and economic damage has been severe to everyone in the U.S. and no doubt will continue into the future. The New York Times said today there were more deaths than in World War I and World War II combined.

We are riding out the virus quarantine like every American staying home and keeping in touch with our families and friends and clients as best we can.

Ingrid and I are so thankful that we have survived so far in our long and happy lives and we are looking forward to the future. I'm hoping to take her to Tahiti when we can fly again. We will see.

What more can I say? Ingrid is working on her flowers and I'm trying to get my computer going. So what's new?

We are both looking to the future, even though it's hard to see. We suspect that family and friends will become ever more important as the world changes. Faith and freedom and love will ever be more important as we age. We pray for our country, our president, and all the other countries of the world as they suffer.

We pray most for our young people as they embark on their lives. Go forth with courage, grit and heart. We look forward to meeting you somewhere along the way on the path towards paradise. We guarantee a great ride. Don't let anything hold you back from creating your own great American story!

Fondly,

Ingrid and Jack

Dedicated to our sons John and Robert, our daughters-in-law, Jennifer and Vidhya and our grandchildren, Emma, Avery, Brigid , Jaya, Lekh and Shail to help them all go forward in faith to their destiny.

I last picked up a pen on April 3, 2020. Today is May 30, 2021, Memorial Day. 2020 was a very difficult year. I last wrote on April 3, 2020 as Ingrid was recovering from quintuple bypass heart surgery. Unfortunately we found soon after that she had received a diagnosis of severe stage 4 inoperable liver cancer. We decided not to take the option on a new drug trial. Ingrid did not want the potential side effects. We heard of a doctor in New York that specialized in radiation surgery, Dr. Lieberman. We interviewed him, liked him and went into New York to 37th and Broadway, about 25 times between July and December of 2020. Ingrid and I would drive in together and I would help her walk to the radiation area.

We tried hard but we had to stop treatment in November 2020. Ingrid spent the last days of her life at home, the place that she truly loved, until December 18th when she passed away at Morristown Memorial Hospital. She fought until the end living in the home she created surrounded by the family she loved so much. Everyone that knew her loved her. We were married 58 years. She was 80 years old and Dr. Lieberman said she looked 60. She skied, played tennis and ran most of her life. She worked out until two weeks before her death.

She was the most incredible person and woman that I ever met. I always considered myself a very lucky man.

As I look to turn 85 in two weeks, I will have spent 60 years on Wall Street. I know I have been a lucky and fortunate man. Ingrid was truly a gift from God and I loved her with all my heart, soul and being. I thank God for the gift of my life with the most beautiful wife, mother, woman and most precious loving friend. We created our own paradise here on earth and I look forward to seeing her in Paradise again as my tears fall on this page, again.

Love to all,

Jack

Ingrid in Monte Carlo, 1985

We wanted our story to be told in the hope that some of our young generations of Americans will have faith to go forward in an uncertain world. You have to take a chance. Take that risk—work hard—success can be achieved through love, work, enthusiasm, kindness, honesty and integrity. These human notions have made America great in the past and will continue in the future. Kids, have faith. It will take you everywhere! You will be great too!

Love, *Jack*

NOTE:

After Ingrid's passing, the Ingrid R. Kelly Memorial Scholarship Fund was established at Bigs & Littles NYC to provide scholarships for poor and deserving students, in need of financial help to pursue their American dreams in Ingrid's honor. The first six scholarships were provided in May 2021 and will be presented in a Zoom meeting of the Scholarship Committee on June 23, 2021.

Vidhya Kelly is Chief Executive Officer of Bigs & Littles and supervises the Scholarship Committee.

All my love to all who read this and may they look forward to a happy, joyous, warm and loving future, most of all "to love and be loved" in our great country.

Sincerely,

Jack

PS – We had a Zoom Scholarship meeting on June 16th. I thought it was a great success. The six scholarship winners had a chance to speak as did their family members if they wanted. Our grandchildren introduced the winners and were a part of the program. Next year, I hope we will have a physical meeting of everyone in the program.

I spoke of Ingrid's coming to America as an "Au Pair" at the age of 21 for the princely sum of $35.00 a week to care for 5 children in Westchester, and, of course, she would have to take the $189.50 passage fee on the Rotterdam out of her pay.

I turned 85 just two days before the Zoom meeting above. I was coming to work last Wednesday morning and had a tough time walking from the parking place to the office. I collapsed on 48th Street in my son John's arms on Lexington Avenue ending up in the Emergency Room at NYU's Langone Hospital.

I received care and a stent in one artery, 95% blocked. I got out last Monday but have to go back for more work in three days. I'm not done yet, but I am a little slower. Just Barkley and me now at home at Windsong. John and Rob will keep Windsong in the future for the family. Ingrid's and my ashes will be in the lower wild flower field. What happiness we have had together here. What an amazing American Love Story our lives have been. Can't wait for the next chapter!

Love,

Ingrid & Jack

The Kelly Family
(Clockwise: Rob, Ingrid, John, Jack, Jen, Vidhya, Shail, Emma, Lekh, Jaya, Avery, Brigid)

ACKNOWLEDGEMENTS

I would like to thank my parents and my friends and acquaintances who have helped me through these 85 years. I particularly want to thank my sons, John and Rob and daughters-in-law, Vidhya and Jennifer, for helping me in so many ways, especially these past, most difficult two years. Special thanks to Vidhya for collaborating with me on publishing my story. I want to also thank the men and women of the United States Navy and in particular, the sailors on our destroyer forces who sacrifice every day of their lives, making us safe to enjoy our American freedoms. Thanks to the men of the destroyer USS Kenneth D Bailey, that did so much to shape me forever. Mostly I thank my dear wife Ingrid, who had been a stalwart in every way and encouraged me from the beginning to write this story. God love you all.

Jack